Hawk'.

Thank you for raising the perfect Hawk!

Kitty x .

*For the young, stupid and colourful.*

## pink frills

do you remember
when you were little
your pink knickers
had frills on
and now life
doesn't feel so *frilly*?

# she / a city of gods and mothers.

She's a cowgirl
She likes spittin' on her boots
To make 'em shine
She's a witch
I wish her love of the high priestess
Was her love of mine
She's a noose
Hung around her own ambition
She's one wrong reflection
Shy of an addiction
When she's bleeding
She's a painting
Renaissance of the heart
When she's barren
She's a vessel
Carrying broken parts
She's one crayon shy
Of the whole damn colour scope
When she makes you cum
You question your horoscope
She's the sheer wonder
At the end of the night
When the festival ends
And some prick turns on the lights
She's the sobering thought
That turns you soft
She's no mona fucking Lisa
She's Vincent van fucking Gogh
And when she's polite
She's not polite to you

This woman is a shell of herself
And it's all because of you
If she fights
She's gonna bite
'Cos eve bit that apple
With pure fucking delight
And this pain is hereditary
Like a cancer to our joy
She don't want no mummy's lad
*She wants to ride a cowboy!*
In a city of Gods and mothers
She's no bearer of life
She might be an angel in the sheets
But she's no ones wife
She's a woman
Of divine intervention
When she dances under the moon's light
She commands your attention
And if she were to die young
She'd be a tragedy of epic proportions
But if she dies inside herself
It's some cosmic abortion
She's a free spirit
A hostage to the moon
A hero to the sun
She's not my reflection
But from her, I *run*
Towards the light of a thousand women
*She is whoever she wants to be*
In a city of gods and mothers
*SHE* is our destiny.

# 'I'M NOT GAY, BUT I LOVE WOMEN'

*After hearing a young girl say the words: 'I'm not gay, but I love women,' and then rest her head upon her mate's shoulder.*

*I'm not gay but…*
*I love women*
the way they rest their heads upon one another
on the 26 bus
the way one unclogs her kitchen sink
of her best mates sick
without any fuss
the dodgy dealings of tampons
under graffitied doors
the way we nonchalantly say
*my period blood looks like a dead baby*
does yours?
the way I say
*'I haven't seen you in so long'*
to a complete stranger in a bar
to save her of a man we'd all love to run over
with our bird shit stained car
*which we can drive by the way*
you ever noticed women say *thank you*
and not
*get out of my fucking way?*
the effortless hug at the end of the night
the silent
*I love you transaction*
that keeps hope burning bright

the way I have a friend in every woman
for the shared pain we all know
*the way I hate every fucking woman*
for society told me so
the way they continue to bring life into this world
that has made no safe space for them to live
the way they raise their daughters
to regardlessly give
the way I'll comment
*nice tits*
to my flat chested mate
'cos I can see she's shitting it before her first date
the way I ask what his dick looks like
so I can make snide inside jokes
the way she offers me a threesome
and I have to say
*thank you for the kind offer, but I don't do hairy blokes*
and the way women dance and mother and care
the way a man wouldn't even dare
the way I can run into any woman's arms
and feel at home
because she knows as good as me
this world ain't ours to roam
yet we roam regardless
and we do so with joy
have done since we were just little boys
I'm not gay
*but boy*
do I love women.

# HORNY HOLDING

Every time I want to be held
I picture the arms of the earth
How it cradles it oceans
From the depth of its core
How jealous I am of the fucking ocean floor
How every branch holds the other
How from each nest
Comes and goes the mother
I picture the way mountains thrust
Themselves upon the skyline
How I get on my knees each night
And beg such thrusting to be mine
How even the rain caresses our streets
With such a tender fall I wouldn't know
Like how the dewy banks or mountain tops
Must feel when there is snow
I picture our earths' feathers
Being romanced by the wind
Taken on a journey into the unknown
Their chartered territories thinned
And every time I want to be held
I hold myself quite tight
And think of how the day holds its nerve
Before it becomes the night.

# WARM BREAD

I'm scared to fall in love
Not for what you may think
I'm not scared to get my heart broke
Or to commit to years with some random bloke
I ain't afraid of my secrets or past
I couldn't care less if my marriage doesn't last
I'm scared to be in love

*Because I know it will consume me*

Because I love the sun right now
And it feels as though it is inside me
I love to dance
With my whole heavy heart
And I stare at the empty night
And all I see is God's art
*I fucking love warm bread*
it controls my every thought between twelve and one
I love to know my childhood nightmares have gone
I love the English weather
*Good old unpredictability*
I love to stare out at the ocean
and ignore its purpose of tranquility
I love sex on a Monday
Cos that's not normal, right?
I love dinner with mates
That last well into the night
I love to be hated
Some would say it's a kink
Like how big boys

in their big boy pants
Hate the colour pink
I love my mum n dad
I don't think you're supposed to at 23
But I do
I sometimes love my prick of a brother too
I love to pretend to read classic novels in a cafe
'Cos it makes me look a clever twat
I love that my best mate had a dream
Of fucking a street rat
I fucking love country music
More than I love being alive
Which seems a bit dramatic
Until you hear Jason Isbell live

*I'm scared to be in love*
For I am already in love with many things
And they consume me
So if there were to be a man walk into my life
Dear god
Fucking exhume me.

# TWO FINGERS

two fingers can make a woman very happy
they can be separated
and poised in front of ones face
a profanity
or a welcomed disgrace
they could hold something called fire
between them like love
a birthday candle
or cigarette
gods welcome drink from above
they can poise a pen
and write a letter of love or hate
to the government
to their nan
or to their ex best mate
two fingers can measure
two fingers can hurt
two fingers can leave their mark
two fingers can squirt
they can separate and be one finger on two hands
gestured on a bus
to the elderly
or the man with his penis out
and his unfortunate puss
they can of course play the guitar
heaven's strings
heaven's sounds
or the recorder
if you're a parent
and your love knows no bounds
two fingers can make a woman very happy

so why don't you put yours in your mouth
she needs silence with her two fingers to her lips
as those two fingers go south.

## shadow dancer, risk chancer

you diminish yourself
to just a shadow
'cos you're told
that's all you're worth
to be behind the sun
on your ready knees
and be its casting light
a shapely figure on the ground
chalk lines on the dirt
be careful, my love
shadows dance
and the sun sets
get off those ready knees
and
run.

# the history of the heart

they gave you a helmet for your heart
but you didn't wear it
when you drove that hope
head first into the flames
it died
the way Romeo's heart died
when their family feud joined him in the after life
the way a wife folds in two
as bombs befall the city at night
the way Leonardo Da Vinci cried
at Mona's groaning eyes
the way Jesus learnt of Mary's untimely demise
i can imagine the heart of Pompeii
collapsed with its roots
the rubble of a city like 9/11 at my feet
the way a mother's soul splinters
at her son's Nazi uniform
the relief of his death upon their hellish meet
the way Hiroshima explodes in my heart
like caffeine to the soul
of all the darkest parts of humanity
the unkind nature of growing old
the way Lennon was shot
and Martin Luther King stolen
he lies in the killer's grave
his hope woefully swollen
no man with his voice
should have to sing through the dirt
just to be heard by the bees
holding hope captive on its weary knees

the way Andy Warhol painted soup
and Banksy has no name
the way there's ten iPhones in this decade
and we're still on the same contraceptive
that's unbelievably *man* made
the way kids get bombed on their way to school
and it doesn't hurt my heart
like I know it should
like if this fictional character died
or fell on hard imaginary times
like if I stubbed my toe or lost a nail
the way I see a stabbing on the street
and its no greek tragedy
the way I used to think Chlamydia
was the worst thing that could ever happen
in the entire world
but now I know that they
gave you a helmet for your head
but you didn't wear it
so when you drove that bike
head first into the wall
you died
with your mum n dad's heart.

# ASK ALEXA IF SHE HAS WRINKLES

the default setting is to hate myself
to make my tummy sick
because my head is
when all is quiet
and still
god's unholy hour
just before the bin men
but after the one night standers
there isn't much else to do
other than hate myself
or gorge on chocolate
or stalk my ex
or stalk my ex best friend
or stalk my ex's ex best friend
or gorge on salt n vinegar crisps
or look in the mirror and suck it all in
or google plastic surgery
or google *can I go out in the rain after plastic
surgery?'*
or google cheap creams that are *like* plastic surgery
or ask Alexa quietly what botox actually means
or ask Alexa will somebody still love me with wrinkles
or ask Alexa is she has wrinkles
or gorge on toast
or wank until your clit feels ready to drop off
or stare at models on Instagram
or stare at the fat best mate of models on Instagram
or read body positivity quotes on Pinterest
or find your old Alex Turner board on Pinterest

or watch videos of Alex turner moving his hips on
YouTube
or watch videos of Michael Hutchence moving his
hips on YouTube
or wanking and crying because your clit is sore
or wondering why you don't fit into those jeans
or wondering *do we even fucking need jeans*
or gorge on nutella on toast
or do a ten minute ab workout on YouTube
or do a five minute wind down yoga release on
YouTube
or buy lycra on Amazon because you swear you'll use
it
or buy a yoga mat with pugs on from Amazon
or buy a water bottle from Amazon that tracks how
much you drink in a day
or look in the mirror and wonder when the abs will
appear
or look in the mirror and wonder if I have a shit will it
made the abs appear
or gorge on a warm baguette in the dark
or be sick
or be sick
or be sick again
when all is quiet
and still
god's unholy hour
just before the bin men
but after the one night standers
there isn't much else to do
so I hate myself.  (shrug)

## sure (shrug)

Everyone seems so sure of themselves
I'm sure the sun sets
For the chill over my breasts
And I'm quite sure of death
Even thought it ain't happened yet
I'm sure the sky never wants to rain
But sure enough the heavens open
I'm sure joy wanted to be my favourite thing
As sure as I am that a bird is joyless without its wings
Just as sure as I am of the unrelenting sea
I'm pretty sure you fucking fancy me
But surety seems silly
When surely there's more to life than its debris
I'm sure these emotions aren't mine to feel
For they don't say my name when they scream for me
I'm sure I don't want to feel that bad again
I'm so so so sure stupid fucking brain
I'm fairly sure I was born in love
For the warmth around me now
Everyone seems so sure of themselves
And I just don't get how.

## my wife

I'm marrying the sea
'Cos she makes me wetter
Spending the rest of my life with joy
'Cos she suits my style much better
Than the miserable little boy next door
Who's as stale as life after loss
I'm shagging all the wildflowers
And avoiding all the moss
I'm falling in love with my life
Before it's taken from me
I'm loving this fucked up little world I've created
And marrying the god damn beautiful sea.

# HOOVERING

Who stole all the joy from her heart
And made her cry until she was sick
Who took that little girl
In her pretty princess dress
Who would speak of hope and love
With all the reverence of a great poet
And broke her
Like she were just a thing that needed breaking
To make it easier to take to the tip
Or for storage
To make her easier to keep in the house
Under the stairs
Like a collapsible hoover
Who made your daughter
Feel like a collapsible hoover?

# numb / weeping after sex / still numb

You gotta weep after sex
To feel something nowadays
Could have a hot rod up my arse
And I wouldn't feel a tickle
Gotta damn the tears
at their banks
Else from my red eyes
Will the agony trickle
You gotta hug your mum
To remind her your cool
With being alive
Gotta start to believe it
Else from the bottom of my heart
Your self pity
Will be the only thing that survives
You gotta inject ketamine
In your heart
To give it the little boost it needs
Gotta keep pruning the fear
Else from the terror
Will the fear grow
little spiteful weeds
You gotta peg your eyes open
To see what's real
And what's not
Gotta make sure you can feel
What's in front of you
Else from the shadows
Grows the devil's plot.

## girly girl

Can I be a woman first
And then a friend
Or must I be a friend to all women
Or a woman to all my friends

This dress is too girly
Mummy says
*But you are a girl*
I just wish
I didn't have to present myself to the entire fucking
world

As this archetypal girl
Who zips her pants and lips shut
From predators and prey
Forgetting that sex isn't just instinctive
But could also be for play

And when I go to sleep at night
I sleep in my best girl dress
Unzipping myself from the bodybag
Of a woman pretending not to be depressed

Out of the coffin I arise
From a sunken, sodden slumber
With black arms
And tired eyes

Of staring at myself in the mirror
And hating everything I see
Trying to smile and get on with it
And not say *it's too girly.*

## CAN I CALL YOU A GIRL?

Being a girl is
Wearing pink knickers
From the age of two
It's dolls, barbies and prams
And an allergy to 'owt blue
It's being chased in the playground
And kissed on the cheek
It's being pulled to the front of class
But not being allowed to speak
It's having our hair pulled
And flashing knickers doing cartwheels
It's being laughed at for eating
And encouraged to skip meals
It's learning about your body in a book
It's tampons, blood and shame
It's hating yourself
And your father's family name
It's being fingered in a park
And called a slut the next day
It's saying I asked for it
'cos I didn't know what else to say
It's bitches, witches and slags
And hiding who you are
It's being terrified to leave the house
Or being alone at a bar
It's being nothing more than the size you wear
And how you look in bed
It's fat, skinny, plus size
Lies are the only thing we're fed
It's not being allowed to age
But still looking good when we do

And the menopause is a myth
That only affects the few
It's being told to smile
And *cheer up girl*
It's being stuck on a pedestal
And asked to give us a twirl
It's people pleasing
To not cause a scene
And starving yourself in his image
To keep yourself clean
It's ignoring double standards
And remaining holy, white and intact
It's no self worth without a man
And travelling everywhere in packs
It's a six year old girl
By Oxford dictionary's definition
We remain a six year old
For all of our existence
So you can call me a girl
If you treat me like a woman
If you don't use girl as an insult
Then… *welcome to the coven.*

# what being in your 20s feels like

*It feels like everybody has boarded a train*
*And I'm left at the station*
*Like everyone knows the name of heaven*
*And I'm the devil in carnation*

*It's being ignored*
*In the most spectacular way*
*It's almost poetry*
*As I scream into an empty crowd*
*Waiting for them to notice me*

*There's a sense of longing*
*This tedious obsession with belonging*
*And I'm so very fucking homesick*
*So very bitterly, desperately fucking homesick*

*I'm waiting for the tide to come in*
*And come in thick*
*To wash away the sense I've lost my mind*
*Please*
*Oh, fucking please*
*Do not leave me behind.*

# your whole head a blister

All my friends are on antidepressants
Do you know how much that breaks my fucking heart?
How much I yearn for my arms to be good enough
How I wish laughter truly was medicine
'Cos then I could cure them all with a knock knock
joke
And we could go back to being kids
Throwing trainers on the phone line
And getting lost in the hollow
How I wish our bond
Could be the glue that puts you back together
I know you say it makes it easier
I just wish there wasn't something you found so hard
You needed to be medicated
I just fucking wish it didn't have to be like this
You in so much pain
Your whole head a blister
That you must walk miles on every day
I know the pain is unbearable
Like wildfire to the joy
understand I might cry sometimes
I'm never gonna stop telling you knock knock jokes
Incase they turn into medicine one day
The sweet kind that doesn't hurt your tummy
And I'm never gonna stop tightening that bond
In the hopes it might piece you back together
*one bloody glorious and victorious day*
Because I've got so much faith in you
And the kid I know hiding somewhere inside
Throwing trainers on the phone lines
And getting lost in the hollow of your mind.

## do it with heart

We've been growing up together
Now we're gonna grow beside one another
Through the kicking
And the screaming
And the wallow
And the pain
Through the sunny summer nights
And dashing through the rain
Through all the bitterness
And terror
Through the death of our mothers
And the creation of ourselves
We've been growing up together
*Lord*
Don't let us die a part
If you're gonna tear us from this Earth
At least do it with heart.

# BLUE SHACK

Some man lives in my house
I can see him fluttering the shutters from the shore
If I shut my eyes
I can feel myself adorning a wreath upon the door
I build the walls up around me
Blue and white and soft
Voices of the dead surround me
So young, so bold, so lost
A lover in the bed
Steam rising from the coffee pot
We profess our sodden love for one another
Then the night's our sorry lot
A home man made from music
The house of which I'd happily die
If I can live a thousand lives in it first
Kissing good morning the sky.

# INCONVENIENT

The worst part about being single is
There's no one to pick you up from the station
No one to squeeze your back spots
Or capture your elation
When you realise there's another biscuit left in the
packet
No one to help build your flat pack furniture
Because despite being a feminist who makes a racket
I'm useless with bolts and nuts
*That's probably why I'm single*
But I hate that I don't have a designated person to tell
all my weird shit to
Like do flowers know their flowers?
Or how does rain know to be torrential or showers?
I hate coming home to an empty house
When I've had an empty heart all day
But I really fucking love star fishing on my double bed
That doesn't smell of cum
I love that there's no boy in the house I have to kiss
After he's been for a very sweaty run
It's nice to be able to wank in peace
It's really such a fucking treat
There's no one to ask if my arse looks fat in this
*Which it never does by the way*
It's nice to not always feel like a slab of serviceable
sexy meat
Although there's no one to take candid pictures of me
Laughing and looking innocent
No boy's hoodie to steal
Cos they're always the comfiest

No one to recite all your favourite things
Or say on an instagram post how you're the loveliest
Strongest, most inspirational woman he knows
Besides his mum
'Cos his mum's his idol
*Obvs*
No one to argue with when you feel homicidal
No one to shock with the education of how a tampon
actually works
No one to dance with when your feet get that jumping
fever
No one to yell *'fuck you'* to
When he calls you a fucking diva
No corny valentine cards to write sarcastic sex jokes to
No safe dick
Or anyone to hold your hair back when you're sick
Which I know a mate could do
Or I could do myself
Just like the furniture and the wanking
And dancing and instagram posting
it's just a total fucking inconvenience that I'm single
'Cos there's no one to pick me up from the fucking
train station.

# Bad.

Boys would tell me my name is pretty
*So I changed it*
They'd say my eyes were the most beautiful they'd
ever seen
*So I shut them*
Boys would tell me my blonde hair was fit
*So I dyed it blue*
They told me my arse was good
*So I sat down and squished it*
Boys would tell me I was frigid
*So I fucked his best mate*
They'd tell me I was cold
*So I warmed up their heart and ate it*
Boys would tell me I was the best girl in the whole
world
*So I got bad.*

# PRAYING FOR THE DEVIL

But who prays for the devil?
Who wishes her well
To which address do you send her easter card
To heaven or to hell

But who prays for the devil?
Does anyone care how she feels
Or is she just another whinny little bitch
In killer red heels

But who prays for the devil?
Who wishes her a life without sin
If she turns into a good little girl
Does heaven claim that win

But who prays for the devil?
Who is gonna offer her salvation
Is god gonna hold her in his loving arms
Or just offer up penetration

But who
I beg
Who prays for the devil?
Who is waiting for her at those pearly white gates
'Cos you're not telling me
That the devil doesn't have any mates

So who prays for the devil?
Is it our duty as women to kneel
Do we set the table with ripe young men for her
And tuck into our last meal

*I* will pray for the devil
And think of her fondly and often
Waiting for her in heaven
From my womanly shaped coffin.

## human art.

I wake up and have a piss. Through my bleary eyes, I know I
should now wash my face and go make some breakfast.
Then I know I should eat it and drink some water and
inevitably shit it all out. Then I know I need to get dressed
and probably brush my hair. I know I should go be a
functioning member of society and go to work. I know I
should be kind and honest and hard working. I know I
should drive safely on the way home, where I know I should
shower and eat and talk to the ones I love. I know I should
sleep off a hard day and do it all again tomorrow.

I just don't know what to do in-between it all.


In-between the pissing and breakfast, do I paint a picture of
the face I see in the mirror, or the one I want to look back at
me? After shitting, but before I get dressed, do I perform
the melody in my head, or do I let it run raucous around my
mind like a stray dog? Somewhere in-between getting
dressed and leaving the house, do I write these tentative
thoughts down? Do I confine them to paper? Strangling
their vastness into a measly few words. Or at work, when I
am being kind and honest, do I instead be vulgar and vile
and repulse myself so much I unlock the deepest, darkest
parts of myself- discovering that I actually quite fucking like
it.

In-between the car ride and entering the house, do I say all the things my mother could never tell me and her mother never tell her? In-between the shower and talking to the ones I love, do I *scream*?

Do I scream that I don't know what I'm doing? That I know I need to get dressed, but I don't know why. That I know I like to draw, but I don't know why. And that getting dressed and drawing works of art are two things I can do in the very same day and only one of them is rendered productive. **That without a gallery, I am no artist, but without a home, I am still a human. And yet, a human without art is just the same as a gallery with no walls.**

## all the things my mother could never tell me and her mother her

You're about to be petrified
For your whole fucking life
Pubes at seven
Bleed at eleven
Thirteen,
nan goes to heaven

Then you kiss at fourteen
Get pissed at fifteen
*What's so fucking sweet about sweet sixteen?*
Eighteen and you're legal
You're now fresh meat
You're *prey*
Nineteen
and they're worried 'bout how much you weigh

You turn twenty before you know it
You've been fucked by the boy next door
Twenty one
And you're a world class fucking whore

You enter the mirage that is your twenties
Suppose the years blend into one another
Skint
Shit job
No car
No house
And now I'm someone's mother

Baby tore me a new arsehole
They don't tell you 'bout that in mother care
No aisle for new anuses
And removal of tit hair

Thirty five and I'm fucked
I'm wondering whether botox truly is morally corrupt
Or whether it's too late to hand my kid back
Of course I love her
I just wanted more for mothers day
Than a fucking live laugh love plaque

All the things my mother could never tell me
And her mother her
I see on my face
In the lines of my fear

You're about to be petrified
For your whole fucking life
You'll never understand the blood you bleed
You'll never understand the equality you'll plead
You will never
Ever
Ever
Understand why your body has been sold for such
greed

You will never understand what order you should put
your skincare on
You will never understand how to sexily put on a
thong
You will never

Ever
Ever
Understand why wanking is wrong

I'm a woman now
Stopped being a girl at seven
Become a woman when I bled at eleven
Grew my heart when nan went to heaven

That first kiss was shit
WKD is hit or miss
And sixteen's only sweet when it's his
Being legal doesn't mean people won't break the law
between your thighs
Being twenty doesn't make you the grand fucking
prize

And that baby that you hate some days
Will grow up with the same fear you had
Of gang rape
stalking
and being sectioned for being mad
When we're not really mental at all
Not. One. Bit.
How can you lock us up for insanity
When it's them that chop us to bits

All the things my mother could never tell me
And her mother her
'Cos she was so fucking scared
*So very fucking scared*

To pass the fear down
To admit defeat
To tell them
to show 'em
No matter how hard we fought
We still don't own the streets

So she made me tough
As I will make her
Of all the things my mother could never tell me

And her mother her
We're free
Seem to be the words we whisper.

# TRAUMA GIRL

this little girl follows me
she hobbles with curly hair
her fairy wings scratch at my nostalgia
i smell her everywhere

each step I take
she is right there
every time I fall down
she's the only one who cares

she skips behind me
with gay pride so bright
her smile scares the dark away
she carries her love in a flight bound kite

everything I do is for her
for she screams the loudest
even when we're both scared
she's always the proudest

and she looks so fucking pretty
*stoic eyes so bright and blue*
you couldn't imagine ever hurting her
and yet still some people do

this little girl follows me
she hobbles with curly hair
this little girl used to be me
*i take her everywhere.*

# GREAT BLOODY BRITAIN

*for all those special occasions where we sing the national anthem.*

Great Britain
Great bloody Britain
Where young women lie in unmarked graves
In ditches not even fit for weeds to grow
And here we have our young women
Left to flourish and thrive
And rot and die

Great Britain
Great bloody Britain
Where any single person with skin not the colour of mine
Divides streets that have parties for people in crowns
And neglects them and hates them
And abuses them until the day they die

Great Britain
Great bloody Britain
Where boats
The kind you get your kids for the summer holidays
Come to our shores
With kids who look just like yours
Only we let those ones drown
Because they don't know the national anthem

Great Britain
Great bloody Britain
Well the anthem certainly ain't that
When the politics of politics takes over from the
politics
When our prime minister is front page news
And it's never for 'owt good
It's never
Ever
Any
Fucking
Good

Great Britain
Great bloody Britain
Where a cup of tea is sold to cure all
And young women lie in unmarked graves
In ditches not even fit for weeds to grow
And here we have our young women
Left to flourish and thrive
And rot and die

Great Britain
Great bloody Britain
May you lie in an unmarked grave
In a ditch not even fit for weeds to grow
And may you flourish
And thrive
And rot
And die
*Great bloody Britain.*

# GOD ON HIS KNEES

I will burn it down
If you don't stop building bridges out of matches
I will make it rain fire
Till kingdom come
If you don't stop pissing gasoline on our anger
I will burn until there is nothing left to burn
And I will burn with that smile that you beg to fucking
see
If you don't stop putting fire in our way
I will make heaven crumble
And God get on his knees
I will make the skies collapse
And the angels play dirty
I will make a holiday out of hell
And a lover outta the devil
I will
burn
it
down
If you don't fucking stop.

# barbie's blood

I always wondered why my Barbie never bled
Smooth legs
Smooth hair
Smooth
*You know what*
That never bled
I could never tell if she was of age to bleed
*'Cos I don't think they released a Barbie in school*
*uniform, did they?*
The man down the road cried *she must've been legal*
Because she had
Smooth legs
Smooth hair
Smooth
*You know what*
That never bled
Am I the freak?
Or is she the freak?
Where would Barbie bleed?
Would blood pour out her eyes
Tears of the disenfranchised
The pain of her sisters gone to the scrapheap
Or charity shop
Or eBay
Separated sisters
Like all those Yazidi women
She must be fucking terrified
*Barbie*
It's not much of a Barbie world nowadays
The pink she wears has been stolen
And now they use it against us

To be too feminine is still a weakness
To be too blue is still wrong
The short skirt she wears has been stolen
Now it's evidence in court
For all the other Barbies
With their smooth legs
Smooth hair
Smooth
*You know what*
That never bled
It ain't much of a Barbie world out there
There's not so much to smile about babe
All those Ken dolls
Expecting open legs that split
Or could snap with one wrist
And smiles that are always smiling
And blue eyes always painted open
And smooth legs
Smooth hair
Smooth
*You know what*
That never bled
I always wondered why my Barbie never bled
Why she always had something to smile about
Always some reason to stand tall
Always dressed with glamour
And without shame
'Cos the world I know Barbie is full of blood
*Every fucking where*
It doesn't just come out of me every month
But we feed the roses with the same blood
We cover our streets with the same blood
We found countries with the same blood

That you don't bleed
Teaching our sons and daughters
That blood only matters when it's coming from the
dead
That Barbie's blood
Is more shameful than the blood of a dead son on the
street
Who doesn't have
Smooth legs
Smooth hair
Smooth
*You know what*
That never bled
I always wondered why my Barbie never bled
Now I know why she's always wearing pink
Not red.

# prowler.

*"after hearing the news that another woman has died at the hands of a 'prowler'- a man known to the police already for prowling the streets at night where she lived.*

They have a word for him
They call him a prowler
Me and my mates call him a wanker
They know he prowls the streets
They see him every night
Yet they don't do 'owt about it
Until my mate is dead

I have a word for her
In fact I have a few
Fucking lovely,
gorgeous
funny
kind
daughter
sister
friend
The best, best, best
Fucking mate in all the land

They have a word for me
They call me a nuisance
Say they can't do 'owt about the prowler
Or peeping tom
Or flasher
I say you've got names for them all
None of which are right

I have a word for them
In fact I have a few
Fucking vile
Scum
Twatrags
Sons
Fathers
Brothers
The lowest, lowest, lowest
Fucking arseholes in all the land

They have a word for him
The man that kills
And rapes
And stalks
And disembodies
They call him misunderstood
Unloved
Neglected

They call him a boy just being a boy at first
Then he's a teenage lad doing teenage lad things
Then he's a little shit that they can't nick
Then he's a prowler
Then he's a peeping tom
Then he's a flasher
Then he's a rapist
Then he's a murderer
Then he's a wanted man
Then he's a convict
Then he's sorry
Then he's sad

The he's ashamed
Then he's lying
Then he's smiling
Then he's hiding
Then he's a man with no name
Who's made hers turn into misery
And ours into victim
After victim
After victim
After prowler
After prowler
After prowler.

## dear prime minister...

Fuck you for prioritising flower beds
Over my mate's mental health
Fuck you for giving yourself a pay rise
And her nurse a pay cut
Fuck you for ignoring women
And calling us all a useless mutt
Fuck you for lying all the fucking time
And fuck you having a face as sour as sucking on a
fucking lime
Fuck you for the poor decisions you make in your 15
bedroom house
Fuck you for being as quiet as a fucking mouse
When your people need you
As a matter of life or fucking death
Fuck you for building a new roundabout
And stealing my mate's breath.

# PARTY PRESCRIPTIONS

I deal out joy
Kiss whoever looks sad
Push the trial of hope
Onto every indie looking lad
I bag up small moments of bliss
And hand 'em out to all my mates
I give strangers free samples
And don't charge a trust rate
Love is free 'round 'ere
That doesn't need to be pushed or pill-ed
Hugs come in clear glass bottles
And fear can't be billed
I try to make life a little easier
For those whose life ain't been easy for them
Powder of friendship and love
Pills of desire for the merry men
I deal out joy
Kiss whoever looks sad
I *am the party prescriptions*
And you're a sad looking lad.

## you forget

when you forget our plans
*i remember*
when you forget the story I told you just last week
*i remember*
when you forget your meds
*i remember*
you screaming in agony on your bathroom floor
*you forget*
you wanted to die
*you forget*
you begged me to take some of the pain away *please*
*you forget*
you were so terrified to die you shivered and shook
and cried for your mummy
*but I remember*
and I could *never forget.*

# THAT BEST MATE OF MINE

The last time there was a heatwave
I was in your mum n dad's bed
Watching tattoo fixers
And looking after your head

It had melted long before the heat
Turned to mush before our bodies did
You realised your head was poison
And I came to know I was a sad kid

I know we bond over how fucked we are
And it's a real treat to have a mate like you
But I just want to take the pain away
And feel like we used to

With *ease*
Remember that!
I haven't felt a light chest in months now
I know your heart aches so fucking much
I just want to take the pain away duck

I want you to know how fucking great you're doing
Even though I can't see you behind that daze of
sertraline
I know you're in there somewhere
*That best mate of mine*

Fuck
I wish I could just rip your heart out
I feel like I could keep it beating

I'd hug it and love it and hold it
Til it stops bleeding

And while I'm at it, let me take your soul
Give you a rest from that heavy head of yours
Didn't your mother tell you
The deepest scars are from such lonely wars

Seeing you in pain makes me cry
I want you to know that
And remember that
The next time you torture yourself
Please ask why

Would you think such horrible things
Why would you hurt yourself like that
I know you can't help it baby
That's what makes it so fucking hard to look at

I wish I wasn't so fucking useless
Was a doctor or a therapist
Or someone who could mend broken spirits
Or knew a good lobotomist

My words seems so fucking pointless
Like an umbrella in a storm
If I can't take the pain away
At least tell me how I can keep you happy and warm

I know you think about leaving
And I really can't blame you
I know how heavy your head gets
But I really fucking love you mate

Please don't go just yet

We have so many more heatwaves
To lie in your mum n dad's bed and sleep
With out heavy heads and weary hearts
Together is all we need
When we need to weep.

# DOCTOR'S HOLD MUSIC

I feel like I'm dying
My head is falling off
But the doctors hold music is surely there to help
I'm sure they're doing it on purpose
Driving me mad
Giving them more work to do
More drugs to give out
More paperwork to fill in
More fucking crazy women whose pain ain't real
I'm sixth in line
Fuck it really hurts
But it's probably just my hormones
The pill
My weight
My ovaries
My period
My weight
My hormones
My hormones
My hormones
I'm fifth in line
The music has picked up a gear
The madness has picked up a gear
I'm fourth in line
I'm third in line
*I keep fucking crying all the fucking time*
Right
It really bloody hurts now
All over
Everywhere

Head to toe
Shoulders to knees
I'm second in line
I calm myself
Don't get too excited
Remember,
It's probably not death
Not just yet
It's probably just my hormones
The pill
My weight
My ovaries
My period
My weight
My hormones
My hormones
My hormones
Hello, doctors surgery, how may I help?

## MATRIMONY

I remember the first time I saw you cry
Then there was a time
When it felt as though you'd never stop
And I just joined you
A matrimony of weeping
Didn't know what else to do
So I just held you
Your emotions seeping
And as I looked into your eyes
And begged you to think of brighter times
I saw your faith leaping
And just for a second
I swear I'd cured you of mortality
Then the fear came creeping
And when I let you go
I feared I'd lost you forever
Wondered if you'd spend your whole life sleeping
But I let you go regardless
Our matrimony gone
Our hearts still beating
And I remembered the first time I saw you cry
And when it felt as though you'd never stop
*weeping.*

# ill stacked kitchen cupboard

your hair fell out with your thoughts
like mugs when you open that ill stacked kitchen
cupboard
tears came when you did with that bloke from work
wouldn't shag again
but occupied a Tuesday
your teeth rotted with your love
like the garden furniture your mum bought in the
winter sale
sworn to the bitter weather
cries left you when she did
the same noise the hand me down car from your
cousin makes
when it starts in the rain
your hair fell out with your thoughts
'cos you'd piled them in your head
like that ill stacked kitchen cupboard.

# the polite way to hate yourself.

At what point will I recognise this skin exactly?
Reckon I'll ever love it?
Got a ball park number?
Date? Time?
Anything will do really.
Just wondering when
-Ish-
Give or take an hour,
I'll stop fucking hating myself?
Would be nice!
You know?
To take a day off,
Or even just an hour!
A minute?
If you're busy
I understand.
I'd just quite like to look in a mirror
And **not** cry, you know?
'Cos I know it can be done
I've *seen* it be done
It's not a fucking myth!
Like the tooth fairy or dinosaurs
I believe privileged white men do it all the time
So I wondered when
*If at all*
I could not think I'm a fat ugly fucking gangly wide obtuse
disgusting slutty frigid awful foul mouthed big hipped wide
bellied twatting short stubby hairy pussy-ed wonky eyed
dirty stinking poor excuse of a fucking hideous vile cunt that
no one would ever like to look at
never mind fuck!
40 years and three hours, was that?
cool.

# BELLYACHE

my belly is sore
it's round and soft
and feels too big for my bones
feels like something inside
is rather desperate to leave
feels stretched over a mound of volcanoes
*a whole fucking city of the exploding bastards*
i hate myself
i eat to comfort the nausea of being alive
there's something about a crumpet
that makes death seem quite timid
so I eat four in the afternoon
and regret all three of them ten minutes later
my head is sore
it's round and soft
and feels too big for my bones
feels like something inside
is rather desperate to leave
feels stretched
i hate myself
i eat to comfort the nausea of being alive.

## smile!

You can hide so much behind a smile
A packet of fags behind those teeth
A disapproving father in those gums of yours
The fucking self loathing foaming at your jaw
The agony, a salt wash in your already bitter mouth
The missing mum in the gap of your last tooth
I swear there's a fucking tiny violin back there in one
of those molars
Is that your recent heartbreak resting on your tonsils?
What's that smell on your breath?
Can I smell how much you fucking hate yourself?
And the torment on your tongue
Pogoing it's way to the roof of your mouth
Like fingernails clawing inside a coffin
And the jealousy amongst the plaque you can never
reach
And the fear of failure on the tip of your red raw
tongue
And the fucking pain of it all in the blood you bleed
when you spit
The blinding red rage seeping between yellow teeth
You can hide so much behind a smile
*But you can't hide it all.*

# THOUGHTS ON MEN'S SPORTS...

*(sorry)*          *(actually, I'm not)*

Why do we pay men in shampoo ads
Millions of pounds to NOT kick a ball in the net
While our nurses can't afford said shampoo
In our God blessed NHS

Running is alright, I suppose
Women are better though
'Cos we've been running away from men
Our whole lives
Do you really enjoy golf lads
Or just being away from your wives

I did go golfing once
And just hunted in the bush for balls
Or was that spoons on a Saturday night
After I'd had too many screwballs

Badminton is just another excuse
For them to get their cocks out
And for *more* old men
To wear *more* white shorts
Because white underwear
Is *clearly* so important in men's sports

F1 needs to calm the fuck down
And cyclists just need to fuck the fuck off
Tennis hurts my fucking neck
Looking at fucking balls

Squash is just middled aged men on their lunch hour
Whacking the shit outta walls

Football is simply who can get the most money
To chase a ball and miss a net
I'm mostly sad
Poor people's football hasn't happened yet

When a woman kicks a ball she's a lioness
But she can't do her job without being kissed by a
bald bloke
Even with the whole world watching
What a fucking joke

Rugby is more about drinking each other's piss
Than will they score, or will they miss
And as for darts
Well fuck me
I've seen more skill
In the delivery of my nan's well timed farts

So, these are my thoughts on men's sports
Since men have so many thoughts on the women's
*Ultimately*
I think the women can do it better
And snooker shouldn't be a sport
F1 is a glorified who's richer contest
And we should ban white shorts.

## tiny little being

i can't believe people think about me
i live in people's tiny little minds
i'm a happy little tiny being
in someone's tiny little mind
and their mind's aren't always happy
but I'm always happy to be in their mind.

## HAPPY VALLEY

they call it happy valley
now it's more of a death mound
dead boys everywhere
they went without a sound
out there
up on that beckoning hill
all these dead boys
who feared the shoes they had to fill
they all go together
cut from the same wood
hanging from the same branch
these poor fucking kids
didn't stand a fucking chance
they call it happy valley
now it's more of a death mound
dead children everywhere
begging to be lost
before they're found.

## MIA.

because to feel this pain
is to know I have loved
and been loved in return
so I will hold on tight to this feeling
like I held on tight to her
while the grief rages through me
and I'm short of breath
and words
and sense
shook to my core
because to feel this pain
is to know I have loved
and been loved in return
love is love is love
and I know it because of her.

# SUIT OF DEATH

*For all her mates.*

You should wear the suit once
Just for your prom
Not her funeral
*Never* her funeral
It should still smell of sourz and sweat
And sweet misses
Not her death
You should have a hip flask in your pocket
And you should toast it to your youth
Not the end of hers
Your mum should not have just picked it up from the
dry cleaners
Only for it to be stained with bitter mortality
*You should wear the suit once.*

# CRYING TO ME

*You used to come crying to me*
About how fucking awful she was
All that mean shit she said to you
About you
Around you
*You used to come crying to me*
Now I hate the thought that you're crying *because* of
me
I cry sometimes because of you
And how you left
And how I didn't want you to
And all the mean shit you probably say about me
And how fucking awful she probably still is to you
But now you're best fucking mates
*Which really fucking hurts, by the way*
And I just know that I could love you more than she
can
I know I can be nicer to you than she is
I know I would be there for you longer than she could
ever be
*You used to come crying to me.*

# ART SHAPED BINOCULARS

I don't know what your favourite song is at the
moment
Or what you're watching on telly
I don't know what made you cry this week
Or last week
Or the week before that
I never saw your flat
I probably pass it every day
Sorry I don't wave
You probably wouldn't want me to wave anyway
I don't know how your mum n dad are
I'd ask after them every week
I still hope they're okay
I still hope *you're* okay
I wonder how your dogs are
Have they learnt any new tricks?
What are you drawing at the moment?
I miss those smart lines of yours
I miss our chats about art
I've never talked art the same since
I've never met someone who saw the world through
the same art shaped binoculars as me
Before you
I doubt I ever will after you
You might hate me
But I just don't hate you
It's as simple as that
You could spit on me as I walk past your flat
And I still wouldn't hate you
You could draw my evil face with your smart lines

Some ugly contortion you'd call art
And I still wouldn't hate you
I kinda want you to know that
'Cos I hate how bitter this all feels
I'm bored of grieving this now
Of grieving *us* now
I really do believe we'll meet again
And I don't think the fact I didn't know what telly you
watched for a few years will matter
I think I'll know why you're crying again
And what music you're listening to
And what you're drawing
And how your sweet mum n dad are doing
I really do hope they're well
I think we'll meet again
And we won't give a shit that we hated each other for
a little bit
I think we'll talk about art like we did when we were
seventeen and we were just art ourselves
Blossoming into the world, finding our place
I think we might make art together again one day
Your smart lines
And my silly little words
I think the bitterness will fade with time
And we'll go back to loving each other
Like silly little kids
I think we should forget about all this
Until we meet again.

## horrid like henry

You're making me want to be bad
Ugly
Vile
Horrid like Henry
You're making me want to be fucking awful to animals
*How bad's that!*
You're making me want to be mean to the elderly
To myself
To my mum
You're making me want to hurt someone
Really
Really
*Really*
Fucking badly
Because you're hurting me.

# THE LAW OF THE RAVE

I can smell the front man from here
Heroin, crisps and sage essential oils
The man must be given his number one
Before he spoils
I love farting at gigs
No one can hear it
Or smell it
Well, sometimes they can smell it
But they never think it's me
They all point fingers at the
Bearded bloke in the band tee
You don't have to worry
If it's gonna be a loud one
Or a quiet one
They're all silent here
I went to a poetry night once
*You can't fart there*
I don't want to watch the gig
Through some teenage twat's snapchat
I want to see how fit the brooding front man is
And the underwhelming drummer
Gently tapping his high hat
I don't want to see how far you can zoom in
On the front man's limp cock
Despite how impressive it looks in 4K definition
I need him in my visual wank bank
So I can dream of fixing every man on the tour bus
Of their smack addiction
I don't want your overpriced cider
thrown all over me mate

Or your piss for that matter
I don't want your cheesy pits in my face
Do men feel so powerful in the mosh
Circus monkeys
Dancing around the open ring
Dislocated elbows
Pushing women over
Do you feel like the mother fucking king
Stop filming
Enjoy the gig
And live in the fucking moment for a change
I sound like a preacher
For a religion no ones heard of yet
But the next time you go to a gig
Fart all you want
Scream out loud
And let me see the fucking band
You stupid fucking crowd!

# BARRY MANILOW IS A FUCKING LIAR

All these lies
Like Barry Manilow
Who didn't write the song I wrote the songs
Like you saying
You're my best, best, best friend
And hating me all along

All these lies
Like the Earth is fucking round
Flat, square, squished to dust
Like you saying
I love you
If needs must

All these lies
We tell our children
Like wish for things you can't afford
And hide the teeth that once clenched onto life
Like you saying
I'd make the most beautiful wife

All these lies
Like it's a habit born at birth
Spurted out the Earth like bitter trees
Like you saying
I only liked you
When you were on your fucking knees

All these lies
That I have swallowed and choked and endured
Like warm water that's been left in the car all day
All these lies
From all these people
Who don't struggle to say

I love you
I hate you
I want you
I need you
I can't stand you
Fuck you

All these lies
Like Barry Manilow
Who didn't write the song I wrote the songs
Like you saying
I can't fucking stand you
Was the truth all along.

<u>night and day.</u>

These photos make me cry
Why do they get to keep hold of you
And why can't I ever touch you again
I look upon these smiling faces
So tender and in love
Thing is
I still have that love
And I'm tender in the way
I don't give it you
Even thought that's all I want to do
How I can still love something
That has said time and time again
They never want to see me for the rest of their days
Is beyond me
I guess it's similar to day and night
Never seen together
Always chasing the other
Opposites in nature
And both bound by tides that can't change them.

# KINDEST MOTHERFUCKER

If something is gonna make me different
Don't be it my hair or my art
Or the way I like 50s music
In my 20-20 style
Don't be it my colour obsession
Or who I choose to kiss
Be it that I'm kind
I'm the kindest motherfucker in all the land
Be it that I'm honest
In this world of lies
Be it that I'm good
In this no good heart of mine
If something is gonna make me different
Be it that I'm nice.

# JUNGLE LOVE

*everything is overgrown*
my love for you
my hatred too
our dastardly beautiful home
*everything is overgrown*
i've never known such light
to cast upon our unrelenting might
under this wicked heart of stone
*everything is overgrown*
i hate these fairytales of blood you tell
the lovers version of Humpty Dumpty fell
i'm not one to moan
*but everything's fucking overgrown.*

# YOUR DAD'S SHAVING FOAM AND MUM'S GILLETTE

Sharon is on the telly shaving
I was excited to own my first razor
I imagine it's how an American kid feels to own their first gun
The adverts for shaving looked a lot more glamorous when I was younger
Smoother, thinner, toned legs
Plopped onto the side of the bath
The slow
Almost *sensual* movement
The blade gliding along foamy skin
Almost palpable in pleasure and relaxation
Not the frenzied, bleeding chore that I know
Leg behind the ear
Whiff of your own scent
*which is always humbling*
Stretching to get to the three stubborn hairs on my big toe
*Because Sharon doesn't have hairy toes*
Or the quick dry shave of the pits over the sink before you go out
Or the conditioner legs
Because dad has ran out of shaving foam
And despite being 23
I'm too young to buy my own
Or the chopping of stray pubes with nail scissors

Or the bumps and lumps and cuts and worries of cancer from all the said razor bumps and lumps and cuts
Because I'm irrational
And a hypochondriac
And too fucking hot in this bastard shower
WILL IT EVER END!
I'm a boil in the bag chicken here Sharon
Where's the fucking spa music coming from?
My hairy arsehole?
The woman didn't have wrinkly skin like mine
I've overcooked myself again, Sharon
Now razor blades aren't quite synonymous with relaxation
More teenage catastrophe
And a failing mental heath system
And I look at those adverts
Of the women shaving already shaved, toned and shapely legs
Slowly gliding down the shin
With a smile on their shaved face
And the spa music
And the pink handled razor
*because our hands wouldn't know how to work a blue handled one*
And the rose petals
And the 2 for 1 offer on lavender scented shaving cream
As though we actually fucking cared about hairy toes
And the candles
*That have always felt a bit much to be honest, Sharon*
And I feel like I've been lied to
*All my fucking life*

By these women who were supposed to raise me
So I could raise a girl if I wanted
And teach myself
So I can teach her
To shave downwards to avoid razor bumps
And shave off the face of any man who won't fuck you
for having pubic hair.

I'm afraid she's not real
It's gutting, *I know*
A figure of my imagination
I will never wrap my arms around
Despite thinking about how it would feel a dozen times
Will never cry on her perfect shoulders
Despite her crying inside me every night
Will never hear the rhyme of her laughter
Despite all the jokes I tell her
But you
And you
And you
You're as real as my nightmares
But much, *much* sweeter
You live in my mind so fondly
I can wrap my arms around you
And what a fucking treat that is
I promise you I will never let you go
*Please never let me go*
And never drop your shoulder
It's the perfect place for my wet sorrow
And as for the laugh
*Fuck me*
It sets my soul on fire
I hope if I have to lose my sight and ears
I will still be lucky enough to feel that laugh echoing down
Thomas Street
Because I can live with never wrapping my arms around her
If I have you
And you
*And you.*

# ODE TO MUGS

*To all the decaf lovers.*

My favourite has a rainbow on it
Says *'a rainbow a day keeps the blues away'*
I'm not sure how true that is
But I love it even if it's lying
My brother has one with a pineapple on
And a fruit themed pun that's not very funny
Mol collects them
And I'm kicking myself that I can't tell you exactly
which one is her favourite
*What a shit mate I am*
The moo one
The flapjack one
The pink one
There's probably a hidden special one
I know she has a favourite in every home she makes
I ask her what's been the best part of her day
She says climbing into bed with a cup of tea
Her sacred hot brew
Her daily dose of calm
The thing that makes every single thing just right
Not to be underestimated
Or snuffed at
Or laughed at
The hot medicine
Prescribed for broken spirits
Making bellies warm
And heads clear
And hearts content
*Happy even*

Such a large task to ask of pottery and water and a
bag full of
*Whatever the fuck is inside a tea bag*
It's no mean feat
The job of a mug
-  the job of a *favourite* mug -
The pure happiness of a human being is relying on it
To provide the warmth
And the clarity
And the happiness
We cannot lap the daily dose of calm out of our
weary, tired hands
The mug - *the favourite mug* - is the only option
And it must be the *favourite*
The rainbow
The pineapple
The flapjack
The pink one
The hidden special one
The mere sight of it feels like home
In my hands
My weary, tired hands
But now I have everything I need between them
And my head clears
And my heart starts to soar
And my smile starts to grow
And my soul starts to ache less
And my spirit starts to come back to life
And my weariness wanes
And my sorrow wanders
And my tired hands start to dance
' And I take a sip
And I am home.

# WOODLAND DISCO

you have an eternity of black.

the deepest
darkest
black
ahead of you.

so while you can hear the bees
ask them how they got their stripes
command the sea
tell you its every secret
ask how the sun can be so cool
in the morning
and yet so warm to see
demand to know how a butterfly
chooses its wings
ask for directions to the fairy wing shop
call upon the mushrooms
that make the woodland floor a disco
for some advice on staying cool
whisper to the stars
just how they shine so bright
do they use a setting spray
or are they hairspraying their godly face
like the best of us
go ask the eagle how she soars
and how I see her roar ripple on the water
request a date with the lily pad
that happens to be greener than our green earth
ask her how she keeps so clean

in this stinkin' pond water world
call, like bird song, for the ravens
and ask them if they miss their colourful feathers
pluck one from their chest
in a ceremonious manner
wear it with pride
and ask the earth

isn't death punishment enough
*can't we die in colour?*

# DIRTY LITTLE FEMINIST

You're a dirty little feminist
As disgusting as your armpits
Mouth like a sewer
Body like a rat
You've got no interest being pretty
Loud mouths should be fat

You're a dirty little feminist
As perverted as a hedonist
Mind of a liar
Lips like fire
You've got no interest looking at me like that
I'll make the night deadly
You dirty fucking bat

You're a dirty little feminist
A loud mouthed specialist
Legs as wide as a bus lane
Arse as fat as a freight train
You've got no interest being smart with me my dear
I am the dealer
And I deal in fear

You're a dirty little fucking feminist
A damn crazy existentialist
Body that's mine
Head to toe a crime
You've got no interest being a woman darling
When it ain't worth a fucking dime.

# DEVIL DRESSED IN DRAG

I wonder what God would think of this
the devil dressed in drag
picking you up from the airport
'cos one of his sheep got bad

am I the holy one now
for loving thy neighbour
and helping a lost soul
am I holier than her
the horse that got bad
and killed her youngest foal

does she sleep at night
or are her dreams filled with terror
for the thought of her youngest child
out in all weather

I wonder what God would think of this
the devil loving the horse's foal
am I holier than her
or just more human in my soul.

# THOU ART NO HOLIER

Thou art no holier
Than the shit on my shoe
Thou art no better than your daughter
The powers that be
Tell me you're a twat
For putting common verse before her

You should try loving your kid
Like you love your God
Should try forgiving those
Who trespass against you
And start being less of a nob

Give us this day
Our daily bread
And let you bathe
In your comeuppance
Deliver you away from the evil
Inside your bones
Or drown your mouth
With your ignorance

And love your baby
Like you love your God
And maybe you will find
Heaven on earth
Thou art no holier
With hatred in your veins
Thou art no worth.

# THE LUNGS OF THIS TOWN

in the lungs of this town
are boys screaming to get out
their fathers may be faceless
but their cries make a sound
and when the howling shriek
of a mother cries
at the sight of her baby boy
with dead rotting eyes
it demands to be felt
to the core of the earth
if we don't start hugging these broken boys
at their beautiful birth
these lungs are on fire
this town is breaking
under the fucking weight
of the fear inside our sons waking
his father is but a reflection
who won't touch the mirror
for fear of the glass shattering
and making things clearer
in the lungs of this town
are boys screaming to get out
and free they will never be
if the only rest these boys get
is in the ground.

## never been spring

there is no poetry for the loneliness
only to say
that there is a hollowness to my bones
a depth as shallow as my toes
when I scream and break my lungs
nobody knows
for as the winter creeps over our shoulders
*it has never been spring in my heart*
the winter nights are long and sordid
no conditions for hope to start
so cold do these conditions grow
i am almost impossible to touch
i don't beg for enveloped arms or believe
you can love somebody too much
enough for me is to feel something
similar to the warmth of spring
on my tongue
i am fed up of there being no poetry in loneliness
but feeling it all year long.

# TULIP SEASON

Tulip season makes me cry
Hopeful buds
Budding in my bedroom
Plucked too soon for greed
Die too young for my pleasure
Am I the Hannibal Lecter
Of flowers?
Will I eat their sweet nectar
Midnight mass for the joyless and poor
Will I let them rot
Like this feeling inside me
Turning my heart green
*Tulip season makes me cry.*

# the way I love being a woman

The way my chest rises
Volcanoes from the heart
And the smoothness at my hips
The way I can shake 'em
Like my mother taught me
The way I can cry and cry
And create my own thunder
The way I live with shame
The perfect rosy tiny on my cheeks
The way I have no fear
To say I love you is like
Sweet honey medicine
In little clear bottles
My grandmother gave out in the war
The way I only have fear at night
Lonely little shadows
On the wall of my great big heart
The way my friends take off their shoes
Mi casa su casa
The way they cry and cry
Releasing thunder in my kitchen
The way my arms fit round them
Just right
The way things go wrong
And yet I can never see the dark
The way I see the light
Only illuminating the beauty in front of me
Things like that
Demand to be seen
The way I'm not too sure
Why I'm here
The way I don't fuckin' care
To be here is such a joy
And joy must not be questioned
*Magic from the soul*
The way I can forget to be happy

But never, ever sad
The way happiness finds me
And the way my body repels the terror
The way I buy flowers
Because I'm not ready to grow life
Just yet
Buds of darling delight
Their scent
The way I hold my own hand
Because it is moulded from my mother's
The way I cry writing this
Thinking about my lovely mother's hands
The way I shake
And sometimes, *I admit*, tremble
At the thought of ever being ready
The way I hold my gnawing stomach
Blossoming from yesterday's feast
Closing my wet, wet eyes
The way I picture buds of darling delight
Inside me with joy
*Magic from the soul*
Their scent tickling me to sleep
The way I imagine them moulding our hands
So they too
One day
Can weep
Over their lovely mother's hands
The way I love being a woman
But love being a daughter some more.

# BUBBLES TO THE SKY

The women in my life
Bring me more joy than bubbles to the sky
They nurse my broken spirit
And release my pain to fly

They dance with me on nights
That are sore to the soul
They fill me with the glory of togetherness
And stop me growing old

They hold me when I can no longer hold myself
Bringing a lightness and a love
They make me the wealthiest woman alive
There's nothing that I would put above

Their compassion, their honour and their devotion
My life feels complete when I'm with them
I'm void of every other emotion

But love and laughter and friendship
From each and every woman
To live without the love of her
Would simply be inhuman.

# IF HOPE WERE A ROCK BAND

Teenage girls are scary, man
They'd do anything for Harry Styles
One slit her wrists
The other one swore her life to the devil
They chase boys with such vengeance
They get what they want
Those pesky girls
I bet teenage girls were the first to believe in Jesus
'Cos those kids believe in anything
With all their heart
Except for themselves
While teenage boys just believe in the highest scoring
footballer
Or maybe the highest scoring shagger
Or maybe the loudest bigot
Whoever screams first
Teenage girls believe in vampires, man
Did you know that
They wanna kiss 'em
Scream they wanna know what true love feels like
As though they don't hand it out for free each day
They're rite horny
I wouldn't leave 'em alone with a sofa
They're imaginative too
I'm pretty sure teenage girls founded Earth
And I'm pretty sure teenage girls will save it too
If hope were a rock band
Teenage girls are the groupies
And fuck me can they scream
They're so passionate, man

Where did that passion go
When did that passion die
If hope were a rock band
Men are the curfew
And woman are the encore
If hope were a rock band
Teenage girls could keep us alive
They'd carve out hope's manifesto onto their young skin
Spend all night making signs
And scream until they lose their voice
And scream some more
And some more
And some more
If hope were a rock band
We'd all know the words
*Believe in getting somewhere*
*And somewhere might just believe in you*
Couldn't get down Deansgate without some punk in a pink t-shirt
With the words
*Too old to die without*
*Too young to live with*
*Hope*
I think the indie fellah on the radio named 'em the next best thing since sliced bread
If hope were a rock band
Teenage girls are the groupies
Keeping us alive.

## the very same

These are the very same eyes
He looked into
As he called me a slut
They are the very same eyes
I saw her leave
The same eyes
That watched you
Slaughter me
The very eyes
I use to see
These are the very same eyes
I use to cry
And boy
Do I use them
They are the very same eyes
That see myself
Shudder
The same eyes that see why
The very eyes
I use
To close.

# CRACKS IN THE CHELSEA

*For my blue star, wherever you are.*

These cracks keep revealing themselves, a mirror to the
romance. The stained mattress of the Chelsea.
The what we'd call:
'Squatter status of it all.'
The eclectic beatniks, high on life's pick n mix. I think we'd
get them help today, I don't think we'd give them a whole
hotel
To roam
And raid
To rebel
And recover.
To create art never imagined before.
To share love never uncovered.
To cheat and to lie and be at life's peril.
To be sick and deranged.
To cut hair and make love.
To piss in cups and spread toys broken across the floor.
To photograph a moment in time-
Where the cracked beings were left cracked and the ones
who claimed to be whole looked down upon the stars's
children and damned them
And damned them
And damned them
The children of war
Of poverty
Of disarray
These children led by the notion of new
And change
And light
Led to believe they had the stars inside them and could
share the delight
In their beauty
In their androgynous flare
In their queendom.

With the streets that disowned them
And the streets that they hustle on
And the streets that they slept on
and sleep with
and sleep for
And the streets that house the buildings they long to call
home.
And the streets that hold corners with boys waiting around
them
To change everything
And cite nothing
To become something
And leave behind anything that reminds them they are with
pain.
That it is inside them.
Living next to their heart
-The best place to be-
-And the worst to be-
Just like those beings.
So close to those strings
So close to snapping them
So close to everything ending and nothing beginning.
To nothing ending and everything beginning.
So close to the girl next door who has a room of white and a
cigarette.
So close to the genius, and not within the heart.
So close to the affair upstairs
And the boy who had a different walk to yours.
So close
So close
*So close to being perfect*
And yet
I can't help but see the cracks
-Not in the people-
But in the walls.
And in these such walls
*The cracked walls*
You can't help but wonder

If these walls house the hearts of the children of the stars
How can the star's children not have cracked hearts?

## robert.

how can art survive
when the artists must die
if they must
like we insist they must
blue star fading
emerald light dwindling
like a silent flame
here I have his photograph
but not his name
i can call it out
but nothing will come forth
between the living mist
and my dying, dying wish
how can art survive
when the artist must.

## LOVE.

Should I die with love
I haven't died at all
Should I die without
I've passed once before

For in this life
If without love
It is but nothing
Like the ocean void of depth
And colour

If without love
In this life
I shall beg for another.

# THE CROSS

I am haunted by the cross that hangs around her neck
The golden chain which swings in the wind
The promise of something better
Spoken at the end of her bed
The nothing betters that have not yet been blessed
The golden chain which swings in the wind
Chain of terror
Chain of vain
The folded photograph crushed into the locket
The love of a child crushed into nothing
The golden chain which swings in the wind
Her golden hair and golden voice
A word of reason, the calming sense
Pain has befriended her more than the locket
I am haunted by the cross that hangs around her neck
For fear it will hang her

## marianne

*To linger on each other's breath*
*At each other's hips*
*And on the end of every word*
*Spoken in silence*
*On each other's fingertips*
*Barely touching, turning static*
*To linger on the way you hold my pain*
*Like it were my hand*
*Palm to palm*
*Tip to tip*
*Gentle pressure*
*Not too quick*
*To linger on the way you say my name*
*Right before you howl*
*And on your parting final breath*
*of this rich dawning night*
*Before we fall to static*
*Marianne*
*You linger*
*Oh, Marianne*

# TWENTY FIVE YEARS

*for mum and dad*

I know that we are just a story
I know that we are just two stories coming together
To make one great novel

I know that our love is just a feeling
That our love for each other
Feels bigger than anything we've ever felt before

I know that our happiness is just a moment in time
And that our happiness together
Is the only time I care about

I know that our faces are just our ancestors
And I know that the only face I would want to see
smiling
Is our together

I know that being alive is a gift
I know that being alive together is more than a gift
It is an offering of breath

I know that we are just a story
I know that we are just two stories coming together
To make one great novel

# THAT'S LIFE

*To all those we've lost to life and all those we've saved with love*

I want to write about human connection
About grown men crying
About a teenage boy holding the hand of his
teacher's widow
About hanging out the window screaming Sinatra in
the rain on the Mancunian way

I want to write about human connection
About how we all dived on a girl we didn't know to
stop her taking a pill she found on the floor
About a father telling his son 'I love you mate'
About a whole campsite running into the sea to save a
dinghy full of kids

I want to write about human connection
About a boy covering a young girl who was stabbed
with his favourite jacket
About training a Ukrainian welder to fight and
sending him directly to the front line to die nobly
About mates breaking kneecaps in exchange for the
trauma he gave her

I want to write about human connection
About a woman going into a ward of AIDS patients to
hold their terrified hands
About knitting a frog 'cos she said she likes frogs
About standing in the warpath of the school shooter
to save your kids

I want to write about human connection
About singing Don't Look Back In Anger into a silent
crowd
About keeping the grave of a baby clean
About washing your best mate 'cos she's too
depressed to do it herself

I want to write about human connection
About how sometimes it doesn't feel very human at all
And others it's so human I could cry
And I do
In these moments
Of human connection that I want to write about
But can never find the words
So instead I cry
And I cry
And cry
For the love of humans.

# WANKING ADVICE AND OTHER THINGS I'D SAY TO MY LITTLE SISTER

*(if I had one)*

Sticking the handle of a razor up your vagina will not
make you cum
But you might cut your hand
Don't wear the t-shirt
If you don't know the band

Your tits itch when you're on your period
Fuck the cinema
Bring your own pick n mix
Shave downwards
Don't suck dirty dick

I want to tell her that music will cure everything
That dancing is better than crack cocaine
But dancing *on* crack cocaine is also pretty good
That you should love your mum n dad like you know
you should

Sticking a black t-shirt pen up your vagina will not
make you cum
But it will make you embarrassed the next time you do
arts n crafts
I want to tell her that taulcing her best mates room at
night
Is absolutely worth the laughs

Wearing black doesn't make you slimmer

Just fucking boring
That when you turn eighteen
The agony starts dawning

It's okay to hate your neighbour
'Cos he's a twat
As is your best friend's boyfriend
He's *definitely* a twat
You're a bit of a twat too
You'll learn soon enough that we're all just twats

Sticking a purple lipstick you best mate got you for
your birthday up your vagina will not make you cum
But it will give you a purple fanny
*A proper brushed peach*
Don't you dear wear a fucking thong to the beach

You will breakdown and probably dye your hair
People will tell you that it'll damage your hair and that
you'll regret it
They're also twats
Forget it

Spending your wage on outfits is a noble pursuit
If you're gonna drive the boys back from the festival
Do not put them in the fucking boot

Sticking a rolling pin up your vagina will not make you
cum
But it might make a good cream pie
Don't buy waterproof mascara
Nothing will stop you if you're gonna cry

Please, please, please
Don't hate yourself
It's such a shit pastime
Please learn from me
Do tequila with lemon
Not lime

And have all the fun you can get
And don't say sorry
Or please, or thank you too often
Say no
And fuck off
*And enjoy every second.*

# SKINT

The next time you feel skint
Think about how it costs nothing to hug
To give one or get one
You're the luckiest girl alive
The richest girl alive to be in someone's arms

The next time you feel sad
Think about how happy you were
Just last week- dancing
You're the luckiest girl alive
The richest girl alive to have two feet on which to dance

The next time you feel hopeless
Think about how hope has surprised you before
and will again
You're the luckiest girl alive
The richest girl alive to have such hopes to dream of

The next time you feel skint
Think about all the laughter that didn't come from money
Whether you've got it or not
You're the luckiest girl alive
You're the richest girl alive
To be hugging
And dancing
And hoping
And laughing
You're the luckiest girl alive
The richest girl alive.

## EVERLONG YEARNING

I craft these words for you
So you can never die
Eternal lifelong misery
No joint hypocritical suicide
I bury these words for you
So you can lay down the spade
A heavy weary head
Full of fears man made
I bury you in these words
So your death is my death
And your life will flow with the page
Like we both did
Past that daunting, haunting age
I carve out all hope in these words
So you can lay yourself down from searching
And you can finally be at rest my dear
From the ever long yearning.

# DEATH MELODY

The only thing that scares me about death
is the thought of never hearing music again.
And then I hear the wail of a grown woman graveside.
And I hear the thud of children's footsteps as they
skip.
And the birds and the bees.
And I hear your regrets poured over me like one
would pour hot milk.
And I hear your laughter in the distance.
And I hear you're doing better now it's been a year.
So, I guess there's even a melody in death.

# BLACK HEARTED STRANGER

Why are you so desperate to label the love I have?
Is it because I have none for you
*My black hearted stranger*
Or does it offend you, my dear?
The way I love to watch a woman dance
And cackle at your expense
Their strength electrifying the room
Of which you ain't welcome
*A black hearted bigot*
Do I offend you?
My very existence
The yearn I have for peace
The desire I have for freedom
*I love your wife*
What a fucking gorgeous smile she has
Does she offend you too?
The way she looks me up and down
Sizing me up against your double bed
The secrets we'd spill on your drool stained pillow
Do you have black pyjamas to match
*That black hearted soul of yours?*
I bet you'd love nothing more than to watch us love
each other
The way you never do
With youthful abandon
And fiery passion
Would you watch?
*Through your black hearted eyes*
The same eyes that watch your baby daughter skip
Does she offend you too?

The way she looks at her dollies
And not at her fucking daddy
*The black hearted stranger*
So desperate to know
If I wanna fuck him
Or his wife
Do I offend you, my dear?
Or do I *excite* you?

# SUNSETS

How do you fall in love with life?
Well you hate it first
You categorically despise it
With all your being
In fact, you don't want it
Don't think you deserve it
Then one day you will look out at the sunset and just
kind of wonder why anything else exists really
And you will want it more than you've ever wanted
anything else before
You still don't think you deserve it
'Cos you don't
But you fucking want it
Need it
Love it
Are addicted to chasing it
The very thought of loving it
And you slowly start to see that
You don't see the point in anything
If you are not in love with life
And its sunsets.

# SPOONS FROM THE TITANIC

*For all those long distanced friends, lovers and family
members and the oceans that divide us.*

The sea should bring people together
Not tear them apart
It should be the catalyst for reunion
Not the catalyst for longing
It should lap up love
Wash up devotion
I should not be dreaming of running across the ocean
that separates us
I want to see your desire looking back at me in the
rock pools
Three crabs
One dead hermit
And you
Amongst the water
I can tolerate being separated by land
That makes sense
Seems biblical to me
To be cut in two by land
By mountains so big people devote their whole lives
to climbing them
By countries so vast they have a president with a
different name to its people
By land so sturdy
It takes one look at us and pisses its pants laughing
*It's just the sea that stands between us*
I declare the way young lovers do
Just the sea
Just the ocean floor

Just the whole world of marine mammals
Just the shark's home
Just the scuba divers and their submarines
Just the crabs
Just the whales
And the starfish
And the plankton
And the titanic
And the spoons from the titanic
And the towels from the titanic
And the human shit from the titanic
And the spleen of the dead man from the titanic
Just the fucking sea that stands between me and you
Between us
Running into each other's arms
Between us
Not collapsing beneath the weight of longing
Between us
Undoing ourselves
Between us
Being the two people, *together*, that we wish to be
They said loving was easy
And I guess it is
If it wasn't for the fucking sea!

# MOSS

pain unites us
such a bitter thing to say
I wish it was love
but we only know that now
'cos of the pain we talk so much about
you used to say
your feet were in the mud
never knew you to complain
then your head went under
grew moss upon your hair
I once thought it was sweet
that life could grow in death
now I know they're no conditions for a kid
such mud in the head
blue skies should be kept above the eyes
mud below the toes
moss upon the watered ground
and love whichever way the water flows

# NATURE'S CHILD

I rage inside
But outside I am nature
I am the ravine that ravishes through the valleys
The weathered ground too tough for your unbroken
boots
The birdsong that makes you rise from your slumber
The nightfall that doesn't fall for long
I am the day that warms with the weather
The swarm of flies that hover over head
The waves that welcome water
The water of which I wave
I am the flightless ground that looks up to the sky in
wonder
The English tarn tucked up in bed
The beauty of the landscape
The landscape of my beauty
I rage inside
But outside I am nature
Ever present
Calming
Dark
Nature.

## joy

I will search for joy until the end of my days. I shall not waste my time seeking love. I shall spend it seeking joy. I endeavour to be a joy to others. I will find joy in the ordinary. I will sleep with joy. I will eat dinner with joy. I will die with joy as I was born. I am joy. It is always with me. Looking after me. Keeping me warm. Keeping me alive.
Joy is what we should live with.
Joy is what we should die for.

## words.

*goodbye for now.*

I am fascinated by words.
And why some words hurt more than others.
And how some mean more when said in a certain way.
How the same words mean different things from
different people.
And how there are hundreds of words for one thing,
And sometimes no words for another.
Compelling are ideas by the words that define them.
Moments captured by words.
Feelings reimagined in words.
Whole worlds founded on words.
I am fascinated by them.
I hope they continue to remain a mystery for as long
as I can use them.

# THE KID IN COLOUR

I fill my life
A canvas with too many colours
A sickly buttery yellow base
Hues of blue as far as the eye can see
*I mourn the base of white*
*Which one was the base of my*
*Beautifully innocent life*
For now all the corners are black
Each mournful edge
Fading into purple cracks
There is an occasional sunset
Over some horrid time
The orange sands of life
Setting over the edges
Of nature's green knife
At the heart
There is pink
Where my girlhood did grow
Where my girlhood did die
Shot down in blades of black glory
The baby blushed hues
Became my sister's story
Out of the ashes of my girlhood
Came the red
Boiling, satin, rotting red
Casting its unholy rage over my every colour
It is hard to see amongst the mess
Where exactly is the wonder
Until you see the green
Just spurting out the black cracks
Some small buds of hope
Some twisted vines of delight
I am the kid in colour
Who mourns her life of white.

Born in 2000, Kitty is a full time colourful cowgirl from outside of Manchester that writes funny telly and funky books. Her work includes the worldwide selling debut novel 'What If Bowie Were A Woman,' and the album she'd write if she could sing- an interactive poetry book called 'Bamboo Til Two.'

When Kitty isn't writing, she can be found in the middle of nowhere on her paddle board, reading a good book by the beach or pretending she lives in the Chelsea Hotel in the 70s.

Kitty is currently working on her debut comedy screenplay: 'Don't Lick The Walls,' which centres around mentally unwell Flynn Starr and her misfit comrades residing in 'The Sad House.' A new and questionable mental health respite facility where she's left unsure if the house is making her better or worse...

Follow Kitty on her journey to getting her show on telly and all the colourful mishaps in-between on instagram:
@kittyriggs_
Short film- @dontlickthewalls_

You can catch Kitty performing at spoken poetry events, performing poems from both her poetry books- check out her instagram or Facebook for more info.

## with thanks to...

Gina Devon, for photographing the front cover.
And Kelly Hodgkinson, for photographing the back- and a
further thanks to both of them for being such wonderful
friends and cheerleaders.

Another huge thank you to all of my friends for the support
you have given this book and my spoken poetry
endeavours. Turning up to every spoken poetry gig is no
mean feat! I love you guys with all my heart.
As do I love my mum and dad. Contrary to my poem 'warm
bread', I do think you should love your mum n dad at all
ages and boy do I bloody love them.

Special thanks to Drew for his continuous support and
joyous belief in all things creative.

Thank you for reading and finding joy and colour in these
poems. I hope you can find joy and colour in your life too.

love,

the kid in colour xx

Printed in Great Britain
by Amazon